Red Cedar, Red Pine

Poems by
Gary Young

BLUE LIGHT PRESS ◆ 1ST WORLD PUBLISHING

1ST WORLD
PUBLISHING

SAN FRANCISCO ◆ FAIRFIELD ◆ DELHI

Winner of the 2021 Blue Light Poetry Prize

Red Cedar, Red Pine

BLUE LIGHT PRESS
www.bluelightpress.com
bluelightpress@aol.com

1ST WORLD PUBLISHING
PO Box 2211
Fairfield, IA 52556
www.1stworldpublishing.com

BOOK & COVER DESIGN
Melanie Gendron
melaniegendron999@gmail.com

COVER PHOTO
Gary Young

INTERIOR ILLUSTRATIONS
Gary Young

AUTHOR PHOTO
Peggy Young

FIRST EDITION

ISBN: 978-1-4218-3521-1

Acknowledgments

Grateful acknowledgment is made to the following magazines where many of these poems previously appeared:

The American Journal of Poetry: "A Buddha large as a mountain," "When I stare into the well," "Two monks in white robes," "At the end of a narrow, cobbled lane"

Chiron Review: "My youngest son considers"

Cloudbank: "In the hills above Kyoto," "Flowers, cups of sake"

I-70 Review: "A mountain, an island," "I write poems with my sons," "The children playing tag"

Miramar: "A plum tree appeared," "Fleeing the oncoming storm"

New Letters: "Yesterday we sat on the bank," "Cranes follow the river north," "It's possible to enter the great Buddha"

Salt: "The temple opens onto a garden"

Spillway: "The house finch is a personable bird"

"My body does not belong to me" originally appeared in *The Eloquent Poem: 128 Contemporary Poems and their Making,* Persea Books, 2019.

"In the hills above Kyoto" is for Peggy, Jake, and Cooper Young

"The temple opens onto a garden" is for Dennis Maloney

"The house finch is a personable bird" is for Christopher Buckley

for Hollis DeLancey, dharma companion

The winds have died, but flowers go on falling.
Birds call, but silence penetrates each song.

– Taigu Ryōkan

Contents

1   The temple opens

2   A Buddha large as a mountain

3   A mountain, an island, an ocean

4   When I stare into the well

5   Cranes follow the river

6   Yesterday we sat

7   Two monks in white robes

8   A killing heat

9   It's possible to enter

10   The children playing tag

11   My youngest son

12   At the end

13   In the hills above Kyoto

14   Fleeing the oncoming storm

15   My body does not belong

16   Flowers, cups of sake

17   I write poems with my sons

18   A plum tree appeared

19   The house finch

20   Last night I fell asleep

23   About the Author

The temple opens onto a garden and a stream, and below a room hung with portraits of thirty-six immortal poets, a frog blurts out a poem of his own. He knows everything he needs to know about immortality. Tadpoles rest in the mud at the bottom of the stream, and a wagtail flitting over the garden leaves a white dropping on the glassy leaf of a gardenia.

A Buddha large as a mountain sits motionless, while the mountain behind it shudders in a warm breeze that rustles the pine, bamboo, and cedar clinging to its slopes.

A mountain, an island, an ocean made of white stones. Red pine, red cedar, and maple on the farther shore. The gate that leads to this garden is locked from the inside. The Buddha waits just beyond.

When I stare into the well beside Buson's grave, rain disturbs the surface of the water. Whose face is reflected there?

Cranes follow the river north toward the mountains at dusk, and though they cry out as they go, we cannot hear them over the roar of the river flooded with this afternoon's rain.

Yesterday we sat on the bank of the Kamo River, laughing and drinking beer. Today, that very spot collapsed into swollen floodwaters. In the temples, there is so much talk about emptiness, and the ground of being. The void in the riverbank is large enough to hold us all.

Two monks in white robes climb to the top of Mount Inari. They pass through 10,000 torii gates and stop at a hundred shrines. At every shrine they empty coins from an offering box into a wooden crate that one of the monks carries on his back. For him, the walk down the mountain is harder than the walk up.

A killing heat beat the birds into silence. A single cicada called from a gingko, but got no reply. At the fish market, mackerel, tuna, and octopus floated in tubs of ice. Vegetables bobbed beside them in the slushy mix. A woman at the stall filled a bag with ice, balanced it on her head, and put both hands to her mouth so she could laugh at herself.

It's possible to enter the Great Buddha of Kamakura, to feel the sheets of bronze from the inside, gaze into the Buddha's head, and linger in 'the interior of the womb'. The metal sings when you strike it with your hand, and you can sense the statue enclosing you. The world falls away, and like the body of an aircraft, the metal skin holds off catastrophe. When you exit at last, there's no telling where you might be.

The children playing tag on the riverbank chase one another beside the swift water, and don't notice the pair of kites snatching sparrows from the bead trees overhead.

My youngest son considers the effect of imaginary numbers on imaginary numbers. His brother ponders the duality of abstraction and specificity, while I wrestle with the concept of essential nature. We are pilgrims. The branch of a willow bounces off its reflection on the surface of a canal. Mallards bob in a murky pond. A crow tears at the body of a mouse on the gray tile roof of a temple.

At the end of a narrow, cobbled lane, crows gorge on sweet fruit at the top of an orange tree, and leave nothing but an empty rind that hangs there like a waning moon.

In the hills above Kyoto, the hut that Buson built on the ruin of Bashō's home still stands. Its thatched roof staves off rain, thunder rattles the paper screens in the windows, bamboo trembles in the wind, and poems are still being written there beside the silent graves.

Fleeing the oncoming storm, a heron, like a hungry ghost, passed so close that his wings lifted the hair on my head.

My body does not belong to me. Lying motionless for an MRI, the magnetic coils grind away, searching for tumors. I imagine little seeds of death floating all around us. The hypnotic machine pulses and whines, and I'm in the monastery, meditating while cicadas electrify the stagnant air. A monk beats on a wooden drum, and the imaging machine speeds up. The monk whispers, still yourself, and the technician says, you're almost through.

Flowers, cups of sake and cans of beer have been left for the dead, and candle stubs rest on rusty iron spikes. New gravestones made of polished granite glisten. Prayers, and the names of the dead have been deeply etched; it seems they will last forever. Higher up the mountain, the graves are older, more elaborate, and near the peak, three emperors and their retinues lie buried. The rain and the moss never tire.

I write poems with my sons, while Buson lies in his grave just a few steps away.

A plum tree appeared between the woods and what's left of the orchard, the seed either spit out, or dropped there in coyote scat. A redwood limb came down in a storm once, and tore the tree in half, but it grew back, and erupts in a cloud of white blossoms every spring. For years I've promised to prune it and rein it in, but I'm too lazy, or too old, and I've let it grow wild. The blossoms last a week, unless a late storm blows in and strips the tree bare.

The house finch is a personable bird. He shares the feeder, and moves if he is nudged. When other birds scatter, he stays put, unperturbed. He sings at sunrise, and he sings at dusk. His song is joyful and reckless. His head is a crimson blaze. That same fire burns in me.

Last night I fell asleep, and in a dream, I wrote a poem. I worked every line into place, and when I'd finished, I woke up, scribbled the poem down in the dark, and went back to sleep. In the morning, I picked up the notepad beside my bed expecting to find the poem, but there was only a single word printed there: *snow*. The authentic self is inarticulate, and there is no end to the excitement of failure.

Hokyoji Soto Zen Temple

About the Author

Gary Young's most recent books are *That's What I Thought,* winner of the Lexi Rudnitsky Editor's Choice Award from Persea Books, and *Precious Mirror,* translations from the Japanese. His books include *Even So: New and Selected Poems; Pleasure; No Other Life,* winner of the William Carlos Williams Award; *Braver Deeds,* winner of the Peregrine Smith Poetry Prize; *The Dream of a Moral Life,* which won the James D. Phelan Award; and *Hands.* He has received grants from the NEH, NEA, and the California Arts Council, among others. In 2009 he received the Shelley Memorial Award from the Poetry Society of America. He teaches creative writing and directs the Cowell Press at UC Santa Cruz.